Animals That Live in the Forest

Black Bears

by JoAnn Early Macken

Reading consultant: Susan Nations, M.Ed.,
author/literacy coach/consultant

WR WEEKLY READER
EARLY LEARNING LIBRARY

Please visit our web site at: www.earlyliteracy.cc
For a free color catalog describing Weekly Reader® Early Learning Library's list
of high-quality books, call 1-877-445-5824 (USA) or 1-800-387-3178 (Canada).
Weekly Reader® Early Learning Library's fax: (414) 336-0164.

Library of Congress Cataloging-in-Publication Data

Macken, JoAnn Early, 1953–
    Black bears / JoAnn Early Macken.
        p. cm. — (Animals that live in the forest)
    Includes bibliographical references and index.
    ISBN 0-8368-4480-7 (lib. bdg.)
    ISBN 0-8368-4487-4 (softcover)
    1. Black bear—Juvenile literature. I. Title.
    QL737.C27M237   2005
    599.78'5—dc22   2004057220

This edition first published in 2005 by
Weekly Reader® Early Learning Library
330 West Olive Street, Suite 100
Milwaukee, WI 53212 USA

Copyright © 2005 by Weekly Reader® Early Learning Library

Art direction: Tammy West
Cover design and page layout: Kami Koenig
Picture research: Diane Laska-Swanke

Picture credits: Cover, p. 11 © Alan & Sandy Carey; p. 5 © Lisa & Mike
Husar/TeamHusar.com; pp. 7, 15, 19 © Tom and Pat Leeson; p. 9 © Tom Ulrich/Visuals
Unlimited; pp. 13, 21 © Dave Welling; p. 17 © Michael H. Francis

Printed in the United States of America

1 2 3 4 5 6 7 8 9 09 08 07 06 05

Note to Educators and Parents

Reading is such an exciting adventure for young children! They are beginning to integrate their oral language skills with written language. To encourage children along the path to early literacy, books must be colorful, engaging, and interesting; they should invite the young reader to explore both the print and the pictures.

Animals That Live in the Forest is a new series designed to help children read about forest creatures. Each book describes a different forest animal's life cycle, eating habits, home, and behavior.

Each book is specially designed to support the young reader in the reading process. The familiar topics are appealing to young children and invite them to read — and re-read — again and again. The full-color photographs and enhanced text further support the student during the reading process.

In addition to serving as wonderful picture books in schools, libraries, homes, and other places where children learn to love reading, these books are specifically intended to be read within an instructional guided reading group. This small group setting allows beginning readers to work with a fluent adult model as they make meaning from the text. After children develop fluency with the text and content, the book can be read independently. Children and adults alike will find these books supportive, engaging, and fun!

— Susan Nations, M.Ed., author, literacy coach,
and consultant in literacy development

Deep in a den under the snow, a bear **cub** cries. It is hungry. Its mother holds the baby close and feeds it milk. Then she goes back to sleep.

Black bears have soft, thick fur. Most black bears are black. Some are brown. Others are lighter colors.

7

Black bears sleep, or **hibernate**, through the coldest months. They live on their fat until the weather turns warmer.

In spring, black bears wake up and search for food. At first, they find green shoots of plants. Later, bears look for nuts and berries.

11

Black bears find their food by its smell. Bears must eat a lot in spring and summer. They must gain weight for another winter.

13

Black bears also eat small animals and insects. They look for insects under rocks and logs. They dig with their claws.

Black bears walk flat
on their feet the way
people do. They
can run faster than
people can.

Young cubs stay with their mothers. When danger is near, a mother bear sends her cub up a tree. It is safer there. She calls it back down when the danger is past.

Some bears gather where there is plenty of food. Most bears spend their days alone. Black bears are at home in the forest.

Glossary

cub — a baby animal such as a bear or a lion

den — a place where a wild animal rests or lives

gather — to meet

hibernate — to go into a deep sleep for a long time

shoots — the new growth of green plants

22

For More Information

Books

Bears. Animals I See at the Zoo (series). JoAnn Early Macken (Weekly Reader Early Learning Library)

Bears and their Dens. Animal Homes (series). Linda Tagliaferro (Capstone Press)

Bears: Paws, Claws, and Jaws. The Wild World of Animals (series). Adele D. Richardson (Bridgestone Books)

Wild Bears. Seymour Simon (SeaStar Books)

Web Sites

North American Bear Center Kids' Area
www.bear.org/Kids/KA_Home.html
Slide shows, sounds, and facts about black bears

Index

About the Author

JoAnn Early Macken is the author of two rhyming picture books, *Sing-Along Song* and *Cats on Judy*, and six other series of nonfiction books for beginning readers. Her poems have appeared in several children's magazines. A graduate of the M.F.A. in Writing for Children and Young Adults program at Vermont College, she lives in Wisconsin with her husband and their two sons. Visit her Web site at www.joannmacken.com.